MW00364394

Time to Pray

Written by Elmer N. Witt • Edited by Mark S. Sengele

Front cover photo: © Milos Jokic/iStockphoto.com
Back cover illustration: © Alex Mathers/iStockphoto.com

Portions originally published © 1960 by Concordia Publishing House

Scripture quotations are from the ESV Bible® (The Holy Bible, English Standard Version®), copyright © 2001 by Crossway Bibles, a publishing ministry of Good News Publishers. Used by permission. All rights reserved.

The quotation marked *LSB* on p. 62 is from *Lutheran Service Book*, copyright © 2006 Concordia Publishing House. All rights reserved.

This publication may be available in braille, in large print, or on cassette tape for the visually impaired. Please allow 8 to 12 weeks for delivery. Write to the Lutheran Blind Mission, 7550 Watson Rd., St. Louis, MO 63119-4409; call toll-free 1-888-215-2455; or visit the Web site: www.blindmission.org

daily prayers
for youth

Time to Pray

By Elmer N. Witt

CONCORDIA PUBLISHING HOUSE · SAINT LOUIS

Contents

Preface

As part of the planning of this book of prayer ideas for youth, hundreds of young people indicated on a questionnaire whether or not they liked written prayers. A majority answered that they did not. At the same time, a larger majority of the same young people acknowledged that they regularly used some kind of book of prayers if and when they prayed.

In a real sense, then, this book grows from another of the dilemmas of Christian youth: the desire to pray from the heart versus the realization that prayer suggestions or ideas are quite helpful. **Time to Pray** is composed of prayers on a large variety of subjects chosen from lists given by youth themselves. It is by no means complete, but it is prepared in the hope and with the prayer that it may help more young people find more **Time to Pray**.

The prayers of this book are, for the most part, original. Wording and style were selected in the desire to make prayers natural and expected in the midst of everyday happenings in the life of youth.

— Elmer N. Witt

Introduction

The ideal life of prayer is a combination of good prayers of today and yesterday with creative prayers from the heart and lips of the individual who is bold in approaching the throne of mercy through our Lord Jesus Christ. For this reason, we encourage the development of your own prayers on the subjects used in this book. You will note that pages 66–67 list "Suggested Prayer Causes," which might well stimulate your daily prayer, and that pages 54–61 offer evening and morning prayers for each day of the week.

Because of topic or wording, some prayers are more subjective, more personal, than others. This is intentional, and it is hoped that the one who uses **Time to Pray** will have other prayers, the Scriptures, and particularly the words of our Lord's Prayer to balance the devotional time of each day.

The holy Lord of heaven and earth, our Savior, Jesus Christ, has not only commanded us to pray and has not only promised to hear us but has also, above all this, promised to help us learn to pray by the inspiration and power of His Holy Spirit, who lives within us. So, in your own words, possibly helped by this book, and in regular use of the Word of God, make the **Time to Pray** in your life the best part of each day.

About Myself

Prayers about me, my goals,
my problems, my joys

Ask, and it will be given to you; seek, and you
will find; knock, and it will be opened to you.
Matthew 7:7

Responsibility

Lord Jesus Christ, You who always have time for individuals, help me as I find my place in life. Enable me to do my own thinking, my own deciding, and my own planning. Make me grateful for the love and advice of others, but lead me to see Your will in my own heart.

Blessed Jesus, I face challenges and opportunities that make me afraid. I know I am weak and sinful. Be my strength, dear Lord. Surround me with Your forgiving love. Make me sure of Your power.

As I grow in accepting responsibility, keep me from pretending to be what I am not. Protect me, dear friend of sinners, from the mistakes of pride and overeagerness. Grant me courage and joy in choices and decisions made in Your holy name. **Amen.**

Thanksgiving

Dear Father in heaven, teach me the meaning of a thankful life. No mind can understand and no lips can adequately tell the boundlessness of Your gifts to me and all people every day.

Make me mindful of the little things of daily life that continually and unnoticed express Your love: a good night's sleep, comfortable shoes, a glass of cold water, a perfect day, the play of children, the good feeling of success, playing a game, or seeing beauty in nature and in those around me.

Make me mindful of Your greatest gifts, dear God: life and breath itself, the wonders of history, the advances of science, the endlessness of music, and the privileges to talk and hear and see. Even more— the knowledge of the forgiveness of all guilt and sin in the perfect life, a peaceful end to life, and certain resurrection in Jesus Christ, my Savior. **Amen.**

Realities of Life

Teach me, O Master, to study the history of my day. Give me understanding as I hear news reports on radio and television and as I read blogs and Web pages.

Do not let me run from the realities of poverty, crime, tragedy, and death that enter the lives of others. Do not let the depressing picture of my world get me down.

Help me evaluate people and events in the light of my Christian values. Help me keep money, prestige, popularity, education, and physical ability in their rightful place. Help me understand Your will concerning world events, the advances of technology, the discoveries of science, the responsibility of government, the words of intellectual leaders, and the everyday lives of families.

Give me, O God of hope, a sense of optimism and courage so that with all Your people in the Church I might live my life so others may know You and Jesus Christ, whom You have sent. **Amen.**

Temptation

God of strength, I have no power in the face of daily temptation. I am continually in danger of forgetting You and Your Word for me. I am constantly able to harm myself and others in speech and desires and action. I am so much inclined not to do the good things I know how to do.

Teach me that my fight is not against any physical enemy but against spiritual agents from the very headquarters of evil. Make me alert to the shrewdness and power of the ever-present devil, prowling like a lion to attack and conquer me.

Clothe me with Your full armor of truth, righteousness, and the Word of God. Give me faith to protect my soul, and send holy angels to guard me in all my ways.

Lord Jesus, You were tempted in every way even as I am; by grace save me from temptation and eternal death through faith in Your name. **Amen**.

Confidence

Lord, You have been good to me all my life. You have blessed me, kept me safe, forgiven me, and guided me. You have surrounded me with parents, friends, teachers, and pastors as well as with freedom, talent, challenges, and opportunities.

But I am overwhelmed, O Lord. I see Your wonderful gifts, and I am afraid of what You and others expect of me. I fear that I will fail.

Make me worthy, O my God. Take away my feelings of guilt and inferiority. Renew me with the assurance of Your forgiveness for all my mistakes and errors. Remind me that You, O Christ, are alive in me through faith. Give me the confidence that the Holy Spirit will continue to work in me throughout my whole life.

When I know You are near to strengthen and to guide, I am able to face my life and do my best. Help me, O Lord. **Amen.**

Failures

Lord, forgive my failures, and help me to stand up under them. Teach me the grace of humility, the virtue of acknowledging my limitations, and the strength of admitting defeat.

Teach me the wisdom of believers in all ages who learned that life is not and cannot be only about success. May Your testing hand of love be the impulse for my trust to grow and my hope to increase.

May I find completeness and joy in the holy life of Christ Jesus. In the face of my failures, give me comfort in His success as my substitute, my Savior, and my everlasting friend. **Amen.**

Improvement

Holy Spirit come from God, forgive me
for being satisfied with myself as I am.

When I am proud of my accomplishments,
show me Your gifts.

When I rely on my own ability,
show me Your power.

When I feel better than others,
show me Your love.

Holy Spirit sent by Christ,
strengthen my feeble faith.

Feed me each day on the Word of God.

With the confidence of my Holy Baptism and the assurance of the Lord's Supper, enlarge my vision and goals in life.

Holy Spirit promised to all believers,
show me the possibilities of improvement.

Open my mind to new ideas and deeper thoughts
through the words and writing of others.

Holy Spirit, source of good, put me at ease with
those around me.

Give me poise and assurance. Make me willing
to work with others for a better world in which to
praise Your name.

Help me, O Spirit, to grow in all things through
Jesus Christ.

Amen.

Conformity

God of wisdom, help me to know the right time to
be different.

As Noah ignored the laughter of the world, so
may I follow Your will in spite of ridicule.

As Joseph resisted the invitation of Potiphar's wife, so may I control the power of sex in my life.

As David accepted the challenge all others shunned, may I meet the fearful decisions of my life.

As Daniel risked his life for the right to worship, so may I grow day by day in my personal devotion.

As Amos fearlessly pointed to the sins and failures of his time, so may I speak for righteousness, justice, and love.

As Elizabeth's baby leaped for joy at the coming of the Lord, so may I find excitement in Your nearness.

As Mary kept those things and pondered them in her heart, so may I take time to meditate on Your love.

As Stephen prayed for those who stoned him, so may I learn the virtue of a forgiving heart.

As Peter was taught not to call anything unclean that You have made clean, so may I conquer prejudice and hatred for Your sake.

As Paul responded eagerly to the battle of Christian life, so may I willingly walk in the Spirit.

As the Son of Man came not to be served but to serve, so may I give of my life, my time, and my money for the physical and spiritual good of others. **Amen.**

The Heart

Teach me, O Lord, that the motives of my heart are the key to my Christian life. Keep me from being shallow or flippant and from getting lost in things that do not count. Empty my heart of selfishness and the desire for evil.

O Savior, by daily remembrance of Your sufferings, Your death, and Your resurrection, make me new within and enable me to love You with all my soul and with all my mind and with all my heart.

Help me, O God, to build a holy temple in my heart, where I may daily worship the Father, give thanks to the Son, and honor the Holy Spirit. **Amen.**

Envy

O God my Savior, preserve me from all envy of the good of others and from every kind of jealousy. Teach me to be thankful for what others have that I have not and to be pleased with what others do that I cannot.

From all greedy grasping of good things for myself without regard for others, good Lord, deliver me.

From a grudging and selfish spirit toward the blessings and accomplishments of others, good Lord, deliver me.

From profiting and advancing myself at the expense of others, good Lord, deliver me.

O Lord Jesus Christ, lifted up on the cross that I may see what it is to love, grant me the desire and power to give myself to You and to all for whom You died. **Amen.**

Poise

Let my entire person be a witness to
Your name, dear Lord.

> **May the clothes I wear
> and how I wear them,**
>
> **the way I sit, or stand, or walk,
> my personal cleanliness and habits,**
>
> **the words I use and how I use them,
> and the places I go and what I do there**
>
> **reflect the honor of my place as a child
> of the Most High God.**

Teach me the merit of being reserved and modest
and the virtue of putting others at ease.

Grant me common sense and good taste in the
choice of friends, food, and clothes, as well as the
wisdom to use my physical features as gifts from
above. Let my restlessness find rest in You and
produce a happy face, kindly speech, pleasant
manners, and a patient heart, and give me grace
to be aware of the needs of others.

As You dwell within me and give me confidence,
help me live at peace with family and friends

and make me a blessing to many; through Jesus Christ, my Savior. **Amen**.

New Dimensions

When I view Your universe, O Creator, I feel so small. My mind and body are limited by size, education, and age. Who am I that You should pay attention to me?

I pray for a bigger vision of Your world and for a chance to see myself in the perspective of all creation.

I pray for a greater understanding of humankind and its problems, goals, and potential.

I pray for a deeper grasp of the best thoughts and philosophies of humankind throughout the ages.

I pray for a keener concern for the tensions and crises of this day and the days that lie before me.

I pray for a better concept of Your wisdom and power as humankind seeks to explore the universe You created.

I pray for a stronger faith in Your Son, my Savior, so that I may more wisely use these new dimensions of life. Hear me for His sake. **Amen**.

Popularity

From all boastfulness, pride,
and self-pomotion,

O God, deliver me.

From the desire to draw attention to myself and to push myself before others,

O God, deliver me.

From all lack of gentleness, courtesy,
and modesty,

O God, deliver me.

Give me grace to learn, O Lord, that it is better to be right than to be popular, better to be pure than to be in demand. Give me wisdom to choose friends whom I can help and who will also be a blessing to me.

When Your mercy and talents in my life bring me to the center of attention, provide the extra power for me to remain humble and thankful. Let me grow daily, good God, in the mind of Christ, and help me always remember that it is better to give than to receive. **Amen**.

Fear Not

Danger by day and evil by night threaten me, O my God. There is so much of my life I cannot predict or control that I am afraid. I fear the known past and the unknown future.

> **Satan daily marks me as his target.**
> **Worldliness creeps in on every side.**
> **My limitations for good are obvious.**
> **Evil remains attractive.**

Support me, Father, in this hour, and convince me of Your power to save. When I hide from You in sin, seek me with overpowering grace. Fill me with the love that throws fear aside and that knows You will neither leave nor fail.

Assure me that neither death nor life,
Nor things present nor things to come,
Nor anything else in all creation,
Will be able to separate me
From Your love, which forgives.

Speak to me with the "Fear not!" that overcomes doubt and makes triumphant faith possible through Jesus Christ, my Savior. **Amen**.

Humor

Lord Jesus, who brought happiness, peace, and hope to all people on earth, relax those who this day are tense, and lift the spirits of all who are depressed.

Help me find the joys of living.

Give me a godly sense of humor to enjoy jokes, cartoons, and clever stories.

Forgive me where I have taken part in off-color humor and in laughter at the expense of others.

Bless the professional performers and witty friends who bring decent fun into my life.

Make me good-natured, even in the morning, and grant me the ability to laugh at myself.

In the joy of knowing You as Savior and Friend, make me ready to share the enthusiasm and happy vigor of youth with the old, the sick, or the lonely. Re-create me daily by Your Spirit so that I may serve You gladly in freshness of body and mind. **Amen**.

Understanding Sex

Dear God the Father, almighty Maker of heaven and earth, I believe that You have made me and all creatures and that You have given me my body, my soul, and all things. Help me to understand what You have given me and to stand in awe, for I am wonderfully made. I forget, dear God, that this body, which I call mine, and the desires that it brings are not to be used selfishly.

Dear Lord Jesus Christ, God's only Son, teach me to understand my attraction to the opposite sex.

Make my eyes, my hands, and my lips express only love that is honest and real. Always live in my body and in my soul so that I may no longer live to myself but for You, who died for me and rose again. By the remembrance of Your holy love, give me strength to do the good that I want and strength not to do the evil that I hate.

Dear Holy Spirit, Lord and giver of life, make me holy within so that I may know the goodness of physical love. In the Good News of forgiveness and through the receiving of the body and blood of my Lord, let me find purity of thought and cleanness of life. Help me to seek and to know love that is deeper than romance and better than mere physical satisfaction.

Without You, O God, I can do nothing. Help me. **Amen**.

Dates

Lord Jesus, broaden the vision of my faith and the influence of Your love so that my entire life may be consistent and sincere.

Especially help me see my recreation and

dates as part of the life I live in the Spirit. Make me sure that You care whom I date, why I date, where I go, and what I do.

In spite of pressures from the devil and my emotions, give me the courage, O Lord, to choose the good and to refuse the evil. May I think, speak, and act as always in Your presence.

Lord Christ, who entered time to save humankind and to live as an example, help me balance the use of years, months, days, and hours, recognizing the eternal importance of each moment. Whether I eat or drink, whether I am at work or play, whether I pray or go on a date, let me live to Your glory. Amen.

The Love of My Life

I cannot hide my desires from You, dear Lord.

You made me to want friendship and contact with others.

You gave me the desire to love and be loved.

Help me understand my longings.

Help me control my thoughts.

Create in me a clean heart, O God, and renew a right spirit within me.

As I look for a life's companion through my dating and friendships, teach me how to choose. Keep me from overemphasizing good looks, physical appearance, social standing, and wealth.

I am a creature made in love; direct my love, dear Father.

As You have loved me and the Church, O Christ, let me find my partner for life.

As You distribute God's gifts, O Spirit, make my desires and attractions holy.

Holy God, show me Your will for my life. **Amen.**

Christian Love
Based on I Corinthians 13

O Lord, my Lord, fill me with Christian love that

looks for a way of being constructive,

is not possessive,

does not cherish inflated ideas
of its own importance,

has good manners,

is not touchy,

does not compile statistics of evil, and

does not gloat over wickedness of others.

O Lord, my Lord, teach me that Christian love

is glad when truth prevails,

knows no limit to endurance,

has no end to its trust,

has no fading of its hope, and

can outlast anything.

O Lord, my Lord, give me the faith that produces
love such as this; through Jesus Christ, my Savior.
Amen.

My Mind

God of wisdom, make me aware of the potential
of my mind. Exercise my ability to think,

understand, evaluate, and decide. Through the discipline of education and the reality of life, help me grow in the discovery of truth.

Comfort those who have lost the full blessing of intellect, and stir up those who fail to use it. Give me the joy of knowing what to learn and how to learn it as well as the added pleasure of sharing knowledge and wisdom with others.

Teach me the rightful place of intellect in Christian doctrine and life. Do not let me confuse a dull mind with a childlike faith. Help me cultivate my best powers to meditate on Your Word and to absorb Your will into my life.

As You make the wisdom of this world look foolish and choose to save all who believe through the simple Gospel, keep me from depending on my reason for the blessings of the Spirit. In the preaching of Christ crucified, may I find all I need for body, soul, and mind. **Amen.**

A Student's Litany

For health and strength of body and mind,

God be praised.

For fun and fellowship with friends already known,

God be praised.

For the discovery of new friends and companions,

God be praised.

For inspiration, knowledge, and challenge gained from books, music, and drama,

God be praised.

For bodily refreshment through recreation and sports,

God be praised.

For travel and the experience of new places,

God be praised.

For the work of the Spirit of God in Word and Sacrament, in the counsel of friends, and in all the experiences of daily life,

God be praised.

For the prospect of achievement, graduation, and the joy of my chosen vocation,

> **God be praised.**

In all my life, through Jesus Christ,

> **God be praised.**

Amen.

Against Ingratitude

For ingratitude to You, who have given me all things and made me for Yourself,

> **Forgive me, good Lord.**

For ingratitude to my relatives, who bear with me so patiently,

> **Forgive me, good Lord.**

For ingratitude to my teachers and friends, who help me on life's way,

> **Forgive me, good Lord.**

Jesus, Savior, as Your mercy and kindness continually surround me, enable me to be rich in thankfulness and praise. Let me show my gratitude each day of each year of my life by doing something for You.

> Give me, O Lord and Master,
> good sense in the use of my time,
> good judgment in choosing friends
> and a future,
> and a good witness to Your place in my
> life. **Amen.**

About My World

Prayers about people and things
in the world around me

If you then, who are evil, know how to give good gifts
to your children, how much more will your Father who
is in heaven give good things to those who ask Him!
Matthew 7:11

The Human Family

O God of love, You have given a new commandment that we should love one another; I pray for those who do not know the satisfaction of being accepted and loved.

I ask Your special mercy

> for the uneducated,
> for the unwanted,
> for the not-too-lovely,
> for those with different-colored skin,
> for the difficult-to-get-along-with,
> for the selfish,
> for the vain,
> for the know-it-alls,
> for the scared,
> for the temperamental,
> for the pessimistic,
> for the cruel,
> for the evil-minded,
> for the sharp-tongued,
> for the gossips, and

for all who by nature, environment, or self are not liked.

Help me, O God, to live in peace with all humankind, to accept as I have been accepted with forgiveness, and to love as I have first been loved through Jesus Christ. **Amen.**

Government and Politicians

You shall have no other gods.

God, help politicians and leaders in government to make You the only God in their lives.

You shall not misuse the name of the Lord your God.

God, help politicians and leaders in government to be sincere when they pray or use Your name.

Remember the Sabbath day by keeping it holy.

God, help politicians and leaders in government to find the time and place to worship You.

Honor your father and your mother.

God, help politicians and leaders in government to remember that they, too, must obey.

You shall not murder.

God, help politicians and leaders in government to have honest respect for all human life.

You shall not commit adultery.

God, help politicians and leaders in government escape temptations to misuse their bodies.

You shall not steal.

God, help politicians and leaders in government to help all people to improve and protect what You have given.

You shall not give false testimony against your neighbor.

God, help politicians and leaders in government to speak only the truth in love.

You shall not covet.

God, help politicians and leaders in government to want what is pure and right.

You shall love the Lord your God.

You shall love your neighbor as yourself.

God, help politicians and leaders in government—and me—to live for You in the forgiving love of Christ. **Amen.**

Peace

Almighty God, You put into the hearts of all people a longing for peace; I ask that according to Your will You would end the misunderstanding, hatred, and fighting among nations.

Keep my country from self-righteousness and foolish boasting and from despising others who have more or less than we have.

Deliver us from wanting to impose our will or way of life on other countries.

Remind us not to trust in science, weapons, or military know-how and strength.

Help my country, O God, and all the nations of the earth to know that You alone are the Lord and that only in You is there hope. Grant us the grace to repent of sin and the desire to listen to Your work. Forgive our evil, heal our spiritual disease, and make us live together in peace.

Prosper and bless all who promote the welfare of the nations of the earth. Make them ministers of Your mercy and messengers of Your love. Make each of us responsible for our brothers and sisters near at home and in different lands, of different cultures and different races.

In war or peace, let Your light shine in me so that all people may see my good works and glorify You, through Jesus Christ, the Prince of Peace. **Amen.**

Parents

Heavenly Father, enable me to show gratitude to my parents, who love me but do not always understand that I am really growing up. Help me understand them, help me accept their wisdom, and help me be a witness to them of Your love.

Keep my parents in health and safety and, according to Your will, give them a long life and carefree days. Protect them from accidents at home and while traveling, from prolonged illness and financial burdens. Make me and all their loved ones a source of comfort and happiness.

Show my parents and me the way to harmony and peace. Guide me so that money, car, work, dates, studies, habits, or family responsibilities do not become more important than our love for one another. Give me the willingness to give in and the courage to apologize. Help me discipline myself so that my laziness, selfishness, noisiness, or other irritations do not become the cause for arguments.

As a child of God, let me daily find power to honor my parents as sent by You, through the patience and obedient love of Jesus Christ, my Lord. **Amen.**

The Good Things

Teach me, God of wisdom, to appreciate whatever is true, honorable, and just, whatever is pure, lovely, and gracious.

Inspire the leaders, craftsmen, and speakers in the world of communications so that through newspapers, television, radio, magazines, and books I may find greater wisdom and deeper truth.

Train the eyes of my mind and spirit on Your world around me so that in nature, physical form, vastness, grandeur, and color I may find joy in beauty.

Open my heart to the goodness of my fellow neighbors and to the rich love of my fellow believers.

May truth, beauty, and friendship in my life serve as a reflection of the truth, beauty, and friendship of God purchased on the cross of Jesus Christ, my Lord. **Amen.**

Those Whom I Do Not Like

Lord Jesus, holy Savior, teach me to pray for those whom I do not like. Remove the mask of my own pride, and permit me to see the worth of those around me. Teach me not to hate those whom You love.

With the wisdom that comes from above, show me that all are not alike and that talents are given to each person according to Your pleasure. Make me respect the desires and needs of those who are above me and below me in age, intellect, personality, and position.

Restore to me the joy of sharing You with all people as well as the godly spirit of returning good for evil. Open to me the treasures of Your mercy so that I may be able to do this in Your blessed name. **Amen.**

Nature

Almighty Maker of all things visible and invisible, the heavens declare Your glory and the earth reveals Your wisdom. I bless Your name for the wonderful products of Your creating love:

> **the courses of stars and light,**
>
> **the colors of flowers and rock,**
>
> **the warming sun and air that give life,**
>
> **the changing seasons, beautiful in order,**
>
> **trees and grain that produce marvelously, and**
>
> **animals for work, companionship, and nourishment.**

I am grateful, Lord, that You support all these things as well as those who work with soil by Your powerful Word, so that seedtime and harvest, summer and winter, and day and night will never stop until the end of time.

As You send rain on the just and the unjust, teach me to love all humankind and hate only evil.

As the sparrow does not fall without You, give me confidence and security.

As the lilies of the field without worrying are blessed and made useful, help me concentrate on Your rich promises.

As the grass flourishes and suddenly fades, teach me to be ready for the end of my days.

Gracious God, feed me with the fruits of the earth, but above all provide me with the Bread of Life from heaven; through Jesus Christ, my Redeemer and Lord. **Amen.**

Advertising

Almighty God, Giver of all desirable gifts, help me not to want all the things that advertisers want me to want.

As mercenary merchandisers and unprincipled promoters work to keep me selfish, vain, and competing with others, send Your balancing Spirit to control my desires. Satisfy my real needs with the peace that the world cannot give.

Help me to live within my means, to find happiness in what others have, and to resist

jealousy and greed. In the face of slogans, pictures, jingles, and fads, may I search first for Your kingdom and Your righteousness with the sureness that all other useful things will be added to my life.

May my love for You lead me to want all good things for my neighbor. **Amen.**

My Wallet

Lord, protect my wallet, not so much from thieves or robbers as from me.

> **May I see my wallet as containing Your gift of love, large or small.**
>
> **May I see these gifts as a trust to be used for good in my own life and in the lives of others.**
>
> **May I grow in understanding the worth of earthly gifts and the wisdom of saving.**
>
> **May I never try to fill my wallet selfishly, dishonestly, or at the expense of others.**
>
> **May I learn to pay what I owe to others, in money as well as in love.**
>
> **May I never love my wallet more than You.**

I ask this, Lord, through the holy, redeeming love of Jesus Christ, my priceless treasure. **Amen.**

Science

Holy Trinity, source of learning, I acknowledge You as Creator of the heavens and the earth and Maker of physical matter and all things living. I am grateful that You have made humankind in Your image, given us power to walk with You, and granted us rule over Your creation.

Bless and keep in Your care all who work in the sciences; give patience and wisdom to researchers, scholars, and those who carefully apply discoveries for the good of humankind. For the work of all predecessors in this field and for those who painstakingly study today, I offer my humble praise, O God.

Give to all people, and especially to students of natural and applied sciences, a rightful sense of stewardship of themselves and of the whole creation. In mercy, enable them to bow before Your superior wisdom and to accept all knowledge as a trust. Make science in all its

developments a useful instrument for Your Holy Church so that Your name may be recognized and Your gift of life known through the cross of Jesus Christ, my Lord. **Amen.**

Sports

Lord, thank You for the fun and excitement of sports.

> **For the energy and endurance of my body,**
>
> **for coordination and control,**
>
> **for patience and persistence,**
>
> **for opportunities to practice and train, and for the help of coaches and friends,**

I am grateful, dear God.

Help me keep my work, learning, and play in balance. Show me in all athletic activities the values of

> **keeping physically fit,**
>
> **working with others,**

striving for a goal,
being honest at all costs,
losing without shame, and
winning without pride.

May I use this body, for which Jesus died, to receive spiritual treasures of forgiveness, peace, and eternal life. **Amen.**

Music

Lord Jesus, source of good and center of my thoughts, I thank You for putting music in my life. I am grateful for the harmony of voices and instruments as well as the pleasing sounds of nature and work in the world around me.

Make the music of yesterday and today a blessing in my saddest hour and in my happiest moment. Keep my interests in rhythm and melody, artist and concert, and listening and performing pleasing in Your sight.

Fill my life, holy Savior, with songs of thankfulness and praise. Develop my appreciation and love for

the hymns and liturgy of the Church. Bless those who provide music as a worshipful setting for hearing and receiving the Word.

Lord Jesus, make my life a song of praise for Your everlasting goodness to me. **Amen.**

Travel

Lord Jesus, Savior and King, who traveled among humankind so that we might know the Father, bless the expanding opportunities for travel in my world. I offer my thanks for the progress of transportation on land, sea, and air. I praise Your name for making such advancement useful to the life and work of Your holy family, the Church.

In Your good pleasure, grant me and others the excitement and joy of visiting new places here in my own country and throughout the world. Make me conscious of past history and the events of today as I enjoy scenery, observe people, and refresh my body and mind in the wonders of Your creation.

With Your powerful right hand, dear Father, protect all who travel, day and night. Keep pilots, engineers, drivers, and all those responsible for service alert and faithful in their routine but skillful work. In Your mercy, avert tragedy on the highway and rail and in the sky. Make us all prepared travelers on the way to everlasting life; through Jesus Christ, who gave His life as a ransom for all. **Amen.**

Spiritual Life of Others

You are a witness, O Lord, to all my thoughts and to all my desires. You know me at my best and see me at my worst.

At my best, Lord, fill me with sympathy and love for those around me. Permit me to recognize the burdens of those who are near and dear. Enable me to respond to the needs of strangers. Give me a growing understanding of sorrow, hunger, loneliness, and poverty in all of the earth.

At my worst, Lord, forgive me for self-centered words and self-satisfying deeds. Forgive me for thinking my problems greater than those of

others. Forgive me for wanting pity, mercy, and patience without a willingness to have pity, mercy, and patience for strangers and friends.

Above all, my Lord, help me see humankind's deepest needs and greatest desires. Keep me from judging and condemning. Help me pray for spiritual health and growth in the lives of those whom I know and those whom I don't know. Make me an instrument of giving hope to them by words and actions that show the life and peace of Jesus Christ, my Savior. **Amen.**

chapter 3

About My Life of Prayer

Prayers for each day beginning with the evening; classic prayers; one-sentence prayers; and a responsive prayer with God

But when you pray, go into your room
and shut the door and pray to your Father
who is in secret. And your Father who sees
in secret will reward you. Matthew 6:6

Saturday Evening

I confess, O God, that I have often turned my back on You, Your Word, and Your Church during the past week. In these hours while darkness covers the earth, I ask forgiveness and mercy for evil done and good untouched.

In this night's sleep and in the refreshment of Your love, prepare me for a new life, a new week, and new worship in the morning. Weary and confused by the changes and chances of this world, may I rest in Your eternal changelessness; through Jesus Christ, my Savior. **Amen.**

Sunday Morning

God of all time and of every place, I lay myself before You in the newness of this holy day. I thank You for the protection of holy angels and the nearness of those whom I love. Fill the hours of this day with the light from above so that all I do and think and say may be useful and kind.

Keep me, O Holy Spirit, from the worship of gods that are untrue. Through the sacred Scriptures and

blessed Sacraments, give me a new desire to call
You my God. In the suffering and death of Jesus,
enable me to accept the mysteries of this life and
of that which is to come. **Amen.**

Sunday Evening

Into Your hands, O Lord, I give my body
and soul and all things. I thank You for the
happiness of this day and especially for
those who by their words, kindness, or
example have helped me. I acknowledge
Your presence and Your blessing through the
preaching of the Word and the worship of
heart and lips. Forgive my sins, and give me
quiet sleep for the sake of the Son of Man,
my Savior. **Amen.**

Monday Morning

I awake in Your name, O Father. Give me
enthusiasm this day to work toward my unfinished
goals and incomplete assignments.

In my dealings with family, friends, and those whom I have not yet learned to love, make me aware that "he who does not love his brother whom he has seen cannot love God whom he has not seen" (1 John 4:20). Mercifully remember _____. Enable me this week to feel that in doing my work I am doing Your will and that in serving others I am serving You; through Jesus Christ, my Lord. **Amen.**

Monday Evening

In these days of youth, when ambition, pleasure, and temptation are so appealing, set my heart on heavenly things. Through simple faith in the reconciling visit of Your Son to earth, may I keep the promises made before Your altar. Give me rest this night for the decisions and work that lie before me. Hear the prayers of all who called on Your name today, and deal mercifully with those who do not pray for themselves. Keep our country from war and my family from sin; through Jesus Christ, my Lord. **Amen.**

Tuesday Morning

I have heard with my ears, O God, the things You did in the days of my father and in times of old (Psalm 44:1). Continue this mercy for all humankind and for me in the day just dawned. Create in me a clean heart for the responsibilities of my work and the relaxation of my play. May the witness of my words and life bring others closer to Your love, which never ends; through Jesus Christ, my Savior. **Amen.**

Tuesday Evening

Almighty Creator, as I review this day and prepare for the new one, grant me patience to endure my failures and humility to outgrow my achievements. Give me the perspective of eternity so that each moment I may know that my real home is with You. Accept my special prayer for _____. Help me store up treasures in heaven so that there my heart may find rest and lasting peace through the hope given me and humankind in the resurrection of Your Son. **Amen.**

Wednesday Morning

O God, whose love and blessings I cannot
measure, make me faithful in my calling this day.
May the work assigned, the opportunities offered,
and the decisions faced be an expression of
my life lived in Jesus Christ. I thank You for the
many young people who are bringing credit to
Your name in schools, colleges, churches, and
communities. Keep me from laziness and pride,
and teach me to watch and pray; through Jesus
Christ, my Lord. **Amen.**

Wednesday Evening

Uncrowd my heart, O God, so that the quiet of
this hour may bring remembrance of Your Word,
Your warning, Your promise, and Your power. Cast
out the devils that have tormented me with fears
and contradictions. Lift up my heart and mind to
learn that the sufferings of this hour are not worth
comparing with the glory that is to come. I ask in
particular for _____. Revive me
through the rest for the body and the renewing
of the Holy Spirit sent by Christ Jesus, my Lord.
Amen.

Thursday Morning

Blessed Savior, who taught us to pray "Thy will be done," give me the desire this day to find and obey Your will. In fun and in disappointment, may I walk humbly and not run from the cost of following You. When I fail to find Your will, give me intelligence and courage to act honestly and to wait patiently. Accept my thanks for food, clothes, health, friends, and for my everlasting fellowship with the saints, for whom You died and rose again. **Amen.**

Thursday Evening

Forgive me, O God, for the pretense and empty ideals of this day. Restore me to truth and unselfishness so that I may find satisfaction in the plain circumstances and the average life that I live. Open my eyes to the possibility of service to neighbors, family, strangers, and friends. Teach me again that the one who gives even a cup of cold water because she is a disciple shall not lose her reward; through Jesus Christ, my Savior. **Amen.**

Friday Morning

Holy Spirit, give me inspiration and power to live this day in harmony with those around me. Help me bear the burden when I am misunderstood. Teach me that all whom I know have fears to face, sins to confess, and problems to solve. I especially remember _____. Hear me, O Spirit, and give me the gift of patience; through Jesus Christ, our Lord. **Amen.**

Friday Evening

O Lord, teach me that I can be forgiven only as I myself forgive. Help me to bear in mind my continued shortcomings and my many sins. As I remember the injuries I have suffered and never deserved, may I also see the kindnesses I have received and never earned as well as the punishments I have deserved and never suffered. Forgive my envy of those who have more in their mind or heart or wallet than I have. May I forgive those who envy me; through the grace of Jesus Christ. **Amen.**

Saturday Morning

Lord and Master, Giver of all good things, keep the door of my heart this day so that only love may enter in as well as the door of my lips so that only love may speak through them. What I have said hastily or in error, forgive, and grant me the occasion to correct my mistakes. Let no fear or hope make me false to You or to my neighbor. Revive my body through work and recreation, and make it in all its parts a worthy home for Your Spirit. **Amen.**

Classic Prayers

God grant me the serenity to accept the things I cannot change,
The courage to change the things I can,
And the wisdom to distinguish the one from the other. Amen.

—Reinhold Niebuhr

Lord God, You have called Your servants
to ventures of which we cannot see
the ending, by paths as yet untrodden,
through perils unknown. Give us faith to
go out with good courage, not knowing
where we go but only that Your hand is
leading us and Your love supporting us;
through Jesus Christ, our Lord. Amen.
—(*LSB* 311)

One-Sentence Prayers

O Lord, You know how busy I must be this day; If I
forget You, do not forget me. **Amen.**

> You who have given so much to me,
> give me one thing more—a grateful heart.
> Amen.

O God, help me not to despise or oppose what I
do not understand. **Amen.**

Give me the courage to be either hot or cold,
to stand for something, lest I fall for anything; in
Jesus' name. **Amen.**

I ask, O Father, not for tasks equal to the power I possess but rather for powers equal to the tasks You may set before me. Amen.

Holy Father, in Your mercy hear my anxious prayer; Keep my loved ones who are absent beneath Your care. **Amen.**

Responsive Prayer

O God of life, help me grow in Your Word and wisdom.

> **Jesus said, "All things are possible for one who believes." (Mark 9:23)**

O God of good, help me overcome temptation.

> **Before they call I will answer; while they are yet speaking I will hear[, says the Lord]. (Isaiah 65:24)**

O God of power, make Your rule evident in our world.

> **The LORD is my light and my salvation; whom**

shall I fear? The Lord is the stronghold of my life; of whom shall I be afraid? (Psalm 27:1)

O God of wisdom, direct my generation in the way of peace.

"God opposes the proud, but gives grace to the humble." Submit yourselves therefore to God. (James 4:6–7)

O God of the faithful, give strength to the Church on earth.

Who is it that overcomes the world except the one who believes that Jesus is the Son of God? (1 John 5:5)

O God of truth, help me to live an honest and temperate life.

Seek first the kingdom of God and His righteousness, and all these things will be added to you. (Matthew 6:33)

O God of joy, open our eyes to the blessings and happiness of our day.

The eyes of all look to You, and You give them their food in due season. You open Your hand; You satisfy the desire of every living thing. (Psalm 145:15–16)

Amen.

Suggested Prayer Causes

Use these to build your own daily life of prayer. Add your own on the pages at the back of this book.

> for the Church
> for Christian unity
> for recruitment of professional church workers
> for the decisions of youth
> for personal witnessing
> for mission hospitals
> for fellowship among nations
> for all in authority
> for immigrants
> for workers in lonely places
> for the deaf
> for the blind
> for those without family
> for children
> for the aged
> for those about to join the Church
> for schools, colleges, and universities
> for addicts to harmful habits

for those in mental and emotional stress
for those who mourn
for the terminally ill
for Christian homes
for those about to be married
for industry, labor, and agriculture

chapter 4

About God

Prayers about God as He has made
Himself known in Jesus Christ

God is spirit, and those who worship Him
must worship in spirit and truth. John 4:24

An Act of Faith

I believe that God is a Spirit and that those who worship Him must worship Him in truth (John 4:24).

I believe that God is light and that if I walk in the light, as He is in the light, I have fellowship with Him and all believers (1 John 1:7).

I believe that God is love and that everyone who loves is born of God and knows God (1 John 4:7).

I believe that Jesus is the Son of God, that God has given me eternal life, and that this life is in His Son (1 John 5:11).

I believe that I am a child of God and that this sonship is a gift of His Holy Spirit.

I believe that if I confess my sins, He is faithful and just to forgive my sins (1 John 1:9).

I believe that God speaks to me in His Word and that I should let the Word of Christ dwell in me richly (Colossians 3:16).

I believe that God forgives sin through Holy

Baptism and that the one who believes and is baptized shall be saved.

I believe that Christ's body and blood are truly present along with the bread and wine of the Holy Supper and that I should partake of this Sacrament frequently.

I believe that God actually lives within me and that with Him I conquer sin and death and enter into life.

Glory be to the Father and to the Son and to the Holy Spirit. **Amen.**

Let God Be God

Sharpen my understanding of You, O God, and increase my faith.

I know that Your thoughts are not my thoughts and that Your ways are not my ways (Isaiah 55:8).

I know that as far as heaven is above the earth, so great is Your love to those who fear You (Psalm 103:11).

I know that as far as the east is from the west, so far do You remove my sins from me (Psalm 103:12).

I know I cannot of myself comprehend the breadth and length and height and depth of Your love (Ephesians 3:18–19).

I know that You are able to do far more abundantly than all that I can ask or think (Ephesians 3:20).

Help me by Your love not to want You as less than You truly are.

Help me by Your mercy not to fear that my sins are too great for You to forgive.

Help me through Your grace to accept You as my own so that I may live under You in Your kingdom.

Keep me, holy God, from words and thoughts that make light of spiritual gifts.

Keep me, holy God, from using Your name or Your Word without sincerity.

Keep me, holy God, from forgetting that the Almighty Himself has come to me in the life,

death, resurrection, and continuing presence of my Lord and Savior, Jesus Christ.

O God, I know that You accept me as I am. Help me to receive You. **Amen.**

The Sign of the Cross

May the sign of Your cross, Lord Jesus, made upon the forehead and upon the breast at the time of my Baptism, be the controlling symbol of my life.

May I see in every cross in church, at home, and on the highway a lasting reminder of Your life and death for me.

May the cross tell me of my calling to bear my burden here on earth. May I humbly take up my cross and follow You.

May the cross be a constant witness to the hope within me that You have gone to prepare a place and will come again.

May the sign of the cross made at the time of the Benediction make me sure that Your face

shines upon me and that You will give me peace. **Amen.**

Holy Communion

Lord Jesus, as You say, "Take, eat; this is My body," I stand in awe. How can my lips of sin receive Your holy body?

As You invite, Lord Jesus, "Take, drink; this is My blood," I shake within. This is the blood given and shed for my sin.

Open to me the mystery of the Holy Sacrament, not with human words but with faith from above. Enable me to take body and bread, blood and wine for the welfare of my life.

Keep me from fear of unworthiness by building my trust in Your Word and promise. Stimulate my desire to partake frequently at this heavenly banquet. In remembrance of Your holy, innocent, bitter sufferings and death, may I, through the grace and power of the Holy Supper, witness to Your love until You come. **Amen.**

My Prayer Life

Father in heaven, teach me to pray.

Let me not be satisfied with the words or thoughts of others, but lead me to speak to You myself.

Father in heaven, make Your name holy as I pray.

Set before me the teaching of Your Word so that I may trust the righteousness of Christ and learn to speak.

Father in heaven, let Your kingdom come as I pray.

Impress me with the importance of eternity so that I may carefully place before You my wants of body and spirit.

Father in heaven, let Your will be done as I pray.

Teach me to expect an answer to my prayers, and give me willingness to wait for it. Help me believe that if You spared not Your own Son, You will surely give me all things wise and necessary for life on earth.

Father in heaven, let me forgive as I pray.

Keep me from hypocrisy so that from my heart I may forgive everyone who offends me, irritates me, harms me, or causes me to lose possession and position in life.

Father in heaven, give me the bread I need today, protect me from temptation, and save me from evil, for You have commanded me to pray and have promised to listen; for the sake of Jesus Christ, Your Son, my Lord. **Amen.**

My Witness

O almighty God, I come in the name of Jesus to offer myself as a living witness to Your ways and works. Take my hands and use them; take my lips and speak through them.

Help me witness to my Savior by resisting temptation at work and play, by standing for the truth even when it hurts, and by giving of myself and of what I possess for the well-being of others. Help me especially, dear Lord, to witness when others expect me to be silent

about wrongdoing and when I myself have been guilty of sin.

May I speak humbly of the saving work of Jesus Christ to those whom I meet and see each day. Keep me from being embarrassed to say His name and from fear of ridicule for His sake.

Bless the witness of my daily life so that little children and adults, as well as other young people, may learn of my sure hope in the Lord. In my love and concern for the poor, the lonely, the unwanted, and the sick, may I demonstrate that it is possible for God to live in humankind again through Jesus Christ. **Amen.**

Dependence on God

I am glad to call You Father, O my God.

From the moment of my first breath I acknowledge my need for Your hand of guidance and strength. In the growing turmoil of life I long for Your voice of correction and forgiving love.

Help me to trust in You always. As promises and abilities of loved ones and friends are forgotten or fail, support me with the assurance of Your eternal friendship, wisdom, and might. In the battle with Satan, the evil in the world, and my own self, be my fortress and my sure defense.

Keep all my actions in Your hands, O God, and work Your purpose for my life each day. Teach me to seek Your will in the Holy Bible. Help me benefit from the example and life of my parents, my teachers, my pastor, and others who walk in Your way. Show me that all believers are related to one another in love and are called to serve one another in trouble and in joy.

I am glad to call You Father, O my God, and to call all humankind brothers and sisters in my Lord Jesus Christ. **Amen.**

On Facing Death

O risen Christ, let me learn that You have overcome the threat of death and the power of the grave. In a world filled with accidents, illness,

and crime, let me realize that my appointed day and hour is always near.

Since You faced death for me, make me unafraid. Since You rose again on the third day, assure me of the life that is to come. Since You have promised perfect joy in Your presence forever, teach me to long to be with You.

Use the inevitableness of death as a reminder for me to work at my chosen calling while I have time. Move me to accept the opportunities and challenges of each day to love my neighbor as I love myself. Through the stirring Word of the living Spirit, cleanse me of sin and make me even now one with the saints of all ages; through Him who will remake my earthly body to resemble His own glorious body, Jesus Christ, the Lord. **Amen.**

chapter 5

About the Life of My Lord

Prayers for the great days
in the life of my Lord on earth

And rising very early in the morning, while
t was still dark, [Jesus] departed and went out to
a desolate place, and there He prayed. Mark 1:35

Advent

Dear God of Abraham, Isaac, and Jacob,

> **I thank You for the ancient promises that announced the coming of Your Son;**

Teach me the wonders of Your Word.

Dear God of the wandering Israelites,

> **I thank You for preserving a people of whom the Messiah could be born;**

Teach me the wonder of Your love.

Dear God of all nations,

> **I thank You for preparing the world for the visit of Your Son;**

Teach me the wonder of Your ways.

Dear God, my God,

> **I thank You for paying the price of my sin with the life and death of Your Son and for the assurance that He will come again;**

Teach me the wonder of His name.

Dear God, prepare my mind, body, and spirit for the wonder of Christmas. **Amen.**

The Nativity

Holy blessed Trinity, fill me with the excitement of the birth of the Son of God.

Almighty God, Father of our Lord Jesus Christ, You sent Your Son to be like us and made Him the Son of Man that I might become a son of God. Open my heart to accept this mystery of grace and to trust Your love forevermore.

Lord Jesus Christ, Child of Bethlehem, I am grateful for Your coming to be one with the children of men so that our eyes may see and our ears may hear the goodness of God's forgiving love. Make me worthy to receive this gift and to sing Your praise forever with the joy of the angels.

Holy Spirit of God, against whom no door can be shut, enter the homes of our country and make them holy this day with the pureness and beauty

of love given in the birth of our Savior. Through all we have seen and heard, move us to share the Good News with all humankind.

Holy blessed Trinity, fill me and all the earth with the excitement of the birth of the Son of God. **Amen.**

Epiphany

As men of old followed the star and found the Savior, help me, O God, to follow Your Word and find Him who is the way, the truth, and the life.

As Herod was kept from harming the holy Child, keep me from harming Christ's holy name by my thoughts, my words, or my deeds.

As men from the East brought gold and frankincense and myrrh to the newborn King, grant me the grace to present myself and all that I am and have as a gift to Him.

As Wise Men fell down and worshiped, may every moment of my life be an act of service and love for Your holy Son.

As Mary kept these things and pondered them in her heart, enable me to remember and to love.

As Your Son shines forever as the light of the world, may I show this light to those of my family, my neighborhood, and my world who still live in darkness.

Holy Jesus, come from God, fill me with Your light. **Amen.**

Lent

O Lamb of God, who takes away the sin of the world,
>   **Have mercy upon me.**

You who take away the sin of the world,
>   **Receive my prayer.**

You who sit at the right hand of God the Father,
>   **Have mercy upon me.**

Through the agony in the garden, let me learn to pray for all who are in mental and spiritual conflict.

Through the mocking and crowning with thorns, let me learn to pray for all who are not ashamed of Your name.

Through the carrying of the cross on the way of sorrows, let me learn to pray for those who bear great burdens.

Through the bitter suffering and death, let me learn to pray for forgiveness of all sins.

For You only are holy,

You only are the Lord.

You only, O Christ, with the Holy Spirit,

Are most high in the glory of God the Father.
Amen.

Holy Week

Grant me, Savior, time for quiet thought during these holy days so that I may see and know Your wonderful works in the suffering and death on the cross.

O Son of God,

> speak to me as to the disciples
>> in the Upper Room;
> help me proclaim Your death
>> as I eat the bread and drink the cup;
> through Your loneliness in the garden,
>> comfort me in my fear;
> protect me from denying, betraying,
>> or forsaking You;
> save me when my life
>> condemns You to death;
> forgive my sins, which made
>> the crown of thorns;
> make me willing to carry my cross
>> of problems and disappointments;
> give me a glimpse of what it means
>> to be forsaken by God;
> show me that You were holy in suffering
>> and innocent in dying.

Lord, You did so much for me; now only speak the word, and I will be made spiritually well. May Your wounds heal me, Your virtues complete what is missing in my life, Your death make me alive, and Your cross be my sign of victory. **Amen.**

Easter

O Christ, who on the third day rose again from the dead, train my eyes to see that You have overcome sin, conquered death, and freed me from uselessness. As the soldiers were shaken at Your rising from the tomb, overwhelm me with the truth that death and the grave have no power over me.

O Christ, who on the third day rose again from the dead, discipline my mind to see that You have brought life through Your resurrection. As the disciples were given comfort and joy again in touching Your hands and feet and side, impress me with the truth that You are alive at this moment, that You come to me in the Word, and that You live within me.

O Christ, who on the third day rose again from the dead, awaken my heart to see You bring the victory of unending life in heaven. As the men of Galilee were assured that You would come again, bless me with growing faith during this life and prepare a place for me so that where You are I may always be. **Amen.**

Ascension

O risen Christ, ascended Lord, all power is given to You in heaven and on earth. From Your throne on high,

> rule human hearts in fear and in joy;
> send angel guards to babies and infants
>   and to mothers with child;
> guide the rulers and people
>   of the nations of the earth;
> surround the leaders of labor
>   and industry, the arts and sciences;
> enter the hearts of all who study
>   and teach;
> enliven the routine of office and home;
> give courage to those who serve
>   humankind's bodies and minds
>   through medicine;
> cleanse the Church from error and pride.

O risen Christ, ascended Lord, from Your throne on high, teach me

> that Your nearness means joy,
> that I cannot run from You,
> that You are present when I sin
>   and when I need You most,
> that You still rule, and

that all things work together
for the good of those who love You.

O risen Christ, ascended Lord, be with me always,
even until the end of the world. **Amen.**

Sending of the Holy Spirit

Pentecost

O Holy Spirit, sent by God and forgotten by
humankind, make Your permanent home in my
heart and life.

I believe, O Spirit,
that I cannot,
by anything I have or do,
believe in Jesus Christ,
come to Him as my Lord,
repent of any sin,
pray for any help, or
do good for those in need.
I believe, O Spirit,
that You have singled me out by Your
mercy,
filled me with the Father's love,

**changed me through the Savior's work,
and made me holy in the true faith.**

O Holy Spirit, sent by God and forgotten by humankind, do not forget me and the whole Christian Church on earth. Keep me and all humankind within the reach of Your miraculous Word. Give me thoughts higher than my own thoughts, prayers better than my own prayers, and powers beyond my own powers so that I may be used in the service of God and humankind; through Jesus Christ, my Redeemer. **Amen.**

chapter 6

About My Church

Prayers about the people and programs
of the church I know and love

Consequently, He is able to save to the uttermost
those who draw near to God through Him, since
He always lives to make intercession for them.
Hebrews 7:25

The Church throughout the World

Lord, teach me the expanse of Your love.

Keep me from making You small with my limited mind and faith. Through Your kindness, overcome my narrowness of understanding.

Open my eyes and heart to see the scope of Your work in many ways and in many places. Bless the efforts of the Church to instruct the young, to teach the children, to challenge the youth, to direct the parents, and to sustain the mature wherever Your call may come.

Hearing Your voice through the power of Baptism, the Word, and Holy Communion, may many repent of sin, accept the Savior, and live in love.

Provide for the people unknown to me who do Your work in my name: pastors, teachers, professors, officials, missionaries, deaconesses, DCEs, lay officers and workers, doctors, nurses, and all committed to Your cause. Grant me a greater understanding of their joy in service to God and humankind.

Help me support them with my interest, money, and prayers. May their work and mine always be Yours; through Jesus Christ. **Amen.**

Missions

I pray for the Church, O Father, as it faces a changing world and new tasks. Baptize her again with the Holy Spirit so that all her members may respond quickly to duty, sympathetically to suffering, and loyally to Your Word. Help the Church in every place announce boldly the changeless Gospel of Christ, who redeemed the lost. Fill her with excitement and adventure so that, like her crucified Lord, she may lose herself in the service of humankind.

Mercifully bless the mission of the Church in its work in countries overseas, in new congregations in my own land, in meeting the needs of others, in medical work, and in serving the handicapped and the distressed. Grant me consistently the will to give generously of my money, time, and prayers for this cause of my Lord and Savior.

I pray for the Church, O Father, and humbly ask
that my voice may be added to her witness;
through Jesus Christ, who gave Himself for her.
Amen.

The Unity of the Church

O God, I praise You for making Your Church one
family throughout all the earth. I thank You for
giving us in this day the blessings of the Bible, the
instruction of Your Law, the privilege of worship,
the guidance of faithful pastors, and the great
gifts of Baptism and the Holy Supper.

I confess my own failing to accept the Church as
Your holy family. I confess my sin in looking only
for the externals of size and efficiency. I confess I
have neglected the Church in thought, word, and
deed.

I confess also, O God, the sins of the Church
at large. Forgive our failures and our pride, our
misunderstandings and our stubbornness. Where
we have contributed to the divisions in the
Church, make us truly sorry and willing to change.

O gracious Father, fill Your Church with all truth and all peace. Where it is corrupt, purify it; where it is in error, direct it; where in anything it has failed, reform it. Where it is right, establish it; where it is in need, provide for it; where it is divided, reunite it; for the sake of Him who died and rose again and who prays always for the Church, Your Son, my Lord. **Amen.**

My Congregation

O God, You know the needs of the Church in every place; work mercifully and obviously in my congregation. Stir up our members to see the urgency of its voice in our community and the day-by-day importance of its witness to all humankind.

Teach our congregation to worship honestly and reverently. Lead us to desire the blessing and inspiration of studying the Word. Impress us with the necessity of the Sacraments. Increase devotion in our homes, and deepen our response in stewardship and evangelism. Show us the blessing of our individual differences and the power of our oneness in Your Son.

God our Father, bless the families of our parish; strengthen the faithful; relieve the sick; be near the lonely; arouse those who don't care; comfort those who are emotionally disturbed; lead those who do not yet understand that Your mercy forgives while we are still sinners.

Fill us with love for one another and all humankind through the miraculous power of the Spirit in Christian education. May our schools and organizations for children, youth, and adults be a wholesome disturbance to the easiness of our lives so that we may grow up in all things; through Jesus Christ, our Lord. **Amen.**

My Pastor

Accept my thanks, Lord Jesus, Shepherd and Head of the Church, for the work and life of

_____, my pastor. May I ever see him as one who must account for souls, for he is called by Your Spirit as overseer of my spiritual life.

Give power and wisdom to the work of my pastor, dear Savior, as he

studies Your Word,

reads the wisdom of humankind,

preaches and demonstrates Your love,

wins and instructs those who don't know You,

counsels and guides the wearied and worried,

warns and corrects those who don't care,

and comforts and helps those in trouble.

Give patience and endurance for the routine duties of my pastor, dear Jesus, so that he can

attend meeting after meeting,

not be annoyed by pettiness in the flock of God,

stand up under the pressures of his calling,

respond lovingly to the incessant telephone, and

faithfully meet also the lesser responsibilities.

Give joy and satisfaction in the daily life of my pastor, dear Lord, in his relationships

with his wife and children,

with his neighbors and friends,
with the community and world,
with the congregation and its leaders, and
with me and all young people. Amen.

Christian Youth Ministry

Help the youth of my congregation grow as
Christians, O Lord:

Through worship,
    building a stronger faith in the Holy Trinity;

Through education,
    discovering the will of God for daily life;

Through service,
    responding to the needs of humankind;

Through recreation,
    keeping the joy of Christ in all activities;

Through fellowship,
    finding the power of belonging to others.

Help the youth of my congregation grow as Christians, O Lord, by awakening them to satisfying experiences of careful Bible study. Give them reverence for the Word as well as sympathetic leaders to guide them into Your forgiving love and the excitement of Your gracious will. Lead the adults of my congregation to recognize the potential of the youth and to give them opportunities equal to their energy and faith. Help young people serve other young people and help young people win other young people as they witness to Your first place in their lives.

Help the young people of my congregation grow as Christians, O Lord—beginning with me. **Amen.**

Lay Workers

Revive the life of my congregation, dear Father, with a new and deeper understanding of Your call to every man, woman, young person, and child to serve in love. Keep us from expecting

others to carry our burdens and responsibilities and especially from thinking of Christian pastors, teachers, and other church staff as the only ones responsible before You.

Help all of us, gracious Savior, to learn that as Your love is given freely to all, we all by grace have become kings, priests, and saints in Your sight. Teach us that we are members of one body and that each of us has his or her important function to fulfill. Raise up wise and humble members of the laity, both men and women, who will assume their place as rightful leaders in the spiritual work of the parish, in harmony and cooperation with the pastor.

Make all members of my congregation glad to help in Your work, and grant a spirit of cooperation and godly concern. Show me my place as a young person in my congregation, and equip me to serve with the joy that comes through Jesus Christ. **Amen.**

chapter 7

About the Word of God

Prayers based on the Word of Life
in the Scriptures

If you abide in Me, and My words abide in you, ask
whatever you wish, and it will be done for you.
John 15:7

The Bible

O Holy Spirit, who caused the Scriptures to be written for my learning,

O Holy Spirit, who taught men to write and speak words that are profitable for instruction and correction,

O Holy Spirit, who through the Bible makes humankind spiritually alive in each generation,

Make me love the Bible as the Word of God.

I know, dear God, what I am supposed to do.

I know, O Christ, what is good to do.

I know, O Spirit, what is essential for life.

But, Lord, I forget; I fail. I let the important and unimportant things of this world get in my way. I cannot keep You first in my life.

Awaken in me a new understanding of Your will in the Word. Give me true love for Your voice speaking through prophets, apostles, pastors, teachers, and Christian friends. Through Christ,

show me the comfort, power, and direction I need for my daily life.

Holy Spirit, help me to read, study, understand, and live in the Holy Scriptures. **Amen.**

Heroes of Faith

Lord, let me learn from the prophets.

> **Give me the faith of Abraham,**
> **the courage of Joseph,**
> **the strength of David,**
> **the faithfulness of Daniel,**
> **and the hope of all Old Testament saints,**
> **who believed though they had not seen.**

Lord, let me live in the spirit of the apostles.

> **Give me the boldness of Peter,**
> **the vision of Paul,**
> **the humility of Andrew,**
> **the spiritual depth of John,**
> **and the sureness of all New Testament saints,**
> **who believed because they had seen.**

Lord, help me understand that apostles, prophets, and witnesses of all days are people like me. With my burdens and imperfections, may I, like them, be transformed by Your Spirit and enabled by Your love to live for You.

Lord, make me what I can be through Your mercy and power. **Amen.**

The Lost Sheep
Luke 15:3–7

Keep looking for me, O Lord, until You find me. When I forget and wander from the goodness of Your voice, mercifully lay aside my sin and return me to the security of Your endless love. Convince me that no matter how far I stray or how joyfully I sin, You still come to seek me and save me. Keep looking for me, O Lord, and fill me with strength so that I may sin no more. **Amen.**

Workers in the Vineyard
Matthew 20:1–16

Almighty Creator and Ruler of the world, I thank You for calling me to serve You in the work I do. Help me find satisfaction in the vocation of my choice. Teach me not to consider only material gain or to begrudge Your generosity to others. Enable me to accept unimportant work and tedious detail without complaint as I seek to live my life for Him who became poor for me: Jesus Christ, my Lord. **Amen.**

The Sower
Mark 4:3–20

Lord of all, You who sow the good seed of the Word, grant that my heart will not be so hardened by the artificial busyness of the world that the seed cannot take root, nor be so shallow that the roots cannot go deep, nor be so concerned with the cares and wealth of the world that the seed is choked. Instead, make my heart good ground so that Your Word may be translated into a life of service and love for Your holy name's sake. **Amen.**

The Good Samaritan
Luke 10:25–37

Help me, Savior, not to pass by the suffering and the helpless on the roads of life. Open my eyes to recognize those in need. Cultivate in me a desire to be a friend, to share words of kindness, and to give as You have first given to me. Move me with the promise that whatever is done for those for whom You died, it has been done for You. **Amen.**

The Waiting Women
Matthew 25:1–13

Since I know neither the day nor the hour in which the Son of God will return with all His holy angels, prepare me, O God, with an increasing faith and a profitable life. Keep me from the foolishness of imitating the world and from the disaster of postponing the acceptance of the Word of truth. Make me a humble, helpful, waiting servant of Jesus Christ, my coming Lord. **Amen.**

The Talents
Matthew 25:14–30

Lord, help me use honestly and well this day all the talents You have given me of body and mind, goods and spirit. Set before me the possibilities of growth and improvement so that in using what I have I may receive more. Make me humble in all I can do, and keep me from envy by making me faithful and generous. Since much is expected of the one to whom much has been given, teach me the value and joy of hard work and ready service. This I ask for the sake of Your faithful life and holy death. **Amen.**

The Prayer of Mary
Luke 1:46–47, 49–53

"My soul magnifies the Lord,

and my spirit rejoices in God my Savior. . . .

He who is mighty has done great things for me,

and holy is His name.

And His mercy is for those who fear Him

from generation to generation.

He has shown strength with His arm;

He has scattered the proud in the thoughts of their hearts;

He has brought down the mighty from their thrones

and exalted those of humble estate;

He has filled the hungry with good things,

and the rich He has sent away empty." **Amen.**

The Prayer of Simeon
Luke 2:29–32

"Lord, now You are letting Your servant depart in peace,

according to Your word; for my eyes have seen Your salvation

that You have prepared in the presence of all peoples,

a light for revelation to the Gentiles,

and for glory to Your people Israel." **Amen.**

The Prayer of St. Paul
Ephesians 3:14–19

"For this reason I bow my knees before the Father, from whom every family in heaven and on earth is named, that according to the riches of His glory He may grant you to be strengthened with power through His Spirit in your inner being, so that Christ may dwell in your hearts through faith—that you, being rooted and grounded in love, may have strength to comprehend with all the saints what is the breadth and length and height and depth, and to know the love of Christ that surpasses knowledge, that you may be filled with all the fullness of God." **Amen.**

The Prayer of David

Psalm 51:10–12, 15, 17

"Create in me a clean heart, O God,
     and renew a right spirit within me.

Cast me not away from Your presence,
     and take not Your Holy Spirit from me.

Restore to me the joy of Your salvation,
     and uphold me with a willing spirit.

O Lord, open my lips,
     and my mouth will declare Your praise.

The sacrifices of God are a broken spirit;
     a broken and contrite heart, O God,
      You will not despise." **Amen.**